Spring, 1990

THE MITOTES OF JOHN IGO

NATIONAL POETRY FOUNDATION
POETRY BOOKS

Denis Goacher, *If Hell, Hellas,* 1982
Desmond Egan, *Collected Poems,* 1983
Constance Hunting, *Collected Poems, 1969-1982,* 1983
Michael André Bernstein, *Prima Della Rivoluzione,* 1984
William Corbett, *Collected Poems,* 1984
Carroll F. Terrell, *Smoke and Fire,* 1985
Carroll F. Terrell, *Rod and Lightning,* 1985
Samuel Menashe, *Collected Poems,* 1986
Omar S. Pound, *Arabic and Persian Poems in English,*
  1986
Carl Rakosi, *The Collected Poems,* 1986
Joseph Richey, *Riding the Big Earth,* 1986
Ron Silliman, ed., *In the American Tree,* 1986
Carroll F. Terrell, *Dark and Light,* 1986
Mark Rudman, *By Contraries,* 1987
Barry Goldensohn, *The Marrano,* 1988
Burton Hatlen, *I Wanted to Tell You,* 1988
Thomas Parkinson, *Poems: New and Selected,* 1988

THE MITOTES OF JOHN IGO

"Nothing is secular"
--Michel Quoist

National Poetry Foundation
University of Maine
Orono, Maine 04469

None of these poems has appeared in print anywhere. One early *mitote*, printed in *Advent*, has been dropped from the final manuscript.

Previous publications (all small-press):

GOD OF GARDENS. Cleveland: American Weave, 1962.
A CHAMBER FAUST. Coral Gables: Wake-Brook, 1964.
THE TEMPTED MONK, a Dance Poem. Torrance,
    California: Hors Commerce Press, 1967.
NO HARBOR, ELSE. San Antonio: Et Cetera, 1972.
GOLGOTHA. Et Cetera, 1973.
DAY OF ELEGIES. Et Cetera, 1975.
ALIEN. Austin, Texas: Nortex Press, 1977.
TROPIC OF GEMINI. Peoria: Mullenix Associates, 1981;
    revised edition, 1983.

Copyright © 1989 by John Igo
All rights reserved

Published by The National Poetry Foundation,
University of Maine, Orono, Maine 04469

Library of Congress Catalogue Card Number: 88-63007
ISBN: 0-943373-13-1

for Jude

A NOTE ON MITOTES

Mitotes, according to the instrument accompanying them, are expressive of joy and mirth, or sorrow and gloom. In the festive dances they tap on a tambourine made of a tortoise shell, gourd, or pot; play a cane flute, upon which no melody is played but which is softly blown in time to the chant; and, for rhythm, shake little gourds filled with pebbles or corn. For the dances of sorrow, they play the *cayman*, which emits a harsh, mournful sound.

For the *Mitotes*, always directed by a shaman, they build a great bonfire, and with sad singing, dance around it, taking turns in a circle so it will not cease. Others sit in a circle in sight of the bonfire and utter sad cries.

The dance-chant rises and falls in a melancholy cadence, and occasionally all of them join in the chorus, "Ha-i-yah!"

Father Joseph Solis, 1767

MITOTE OF THE PRESENCES

Ha-i-yah!

The presences are there

Ha-i-yah!

And wait behind
Sounds and signs

Using cups for their drink,
Horizons for their world,
Men cannot perceive them
Or recognize the signs

Or hear their names

> Ants in holes
> See the sky
> As a paleblue disk

> Fish in pools
> See the sky
> As a shimmering ceiling

And caged by the senses,
Those heavy-lidded five eyes of God,
Men lift the cup
And salute the horizon

Ha-i-yah!

MITOTE OF THE VULTURE

As fear grown great becomes myth,
A baleful muse, hawksighted and black,
Lifts away the lying flesh
And bares the constant bone
For mother sun to whiten

Ha-i-yah!

As fear of losing discovers ritual,
There is no flesh that can be laid
Upon flesh to allay the cold--
And the black priest's touch is soft as dew
For mother sun to brighten

Ha-i-yah!

As fear of being lost becomes communion,
The black acolyte's soft offering
Crossed by sand and wind
Is signed by ants and rain
For mother sun to cipher

Ha-i-yah!

As fear of loneliness discovers charity,
Wavering on his tower of silence
The black sun-swan stoops to a companionship
Loosened by the seasons
For mother sun to ripen

Ha-i-yah!

MITOTE OF *ALLA*

There are no edges of escape
Ha-i-yah!

The sky is sometimes the copper foot
That falls upon land as empty,
To the horizon, as a dream-haunted eye

Bones on the sand are old totems,
Letters to spell the sun's seasons,
Sundials of longstilled wandering

All cities are colonial--
Man is an exile hearing, as siren,
The amber voice of evening distance

And thoughts are waxen walls
To hold large space away,
But eyes take root in distance

Flatlands wait, communicant,
For the transforming presence;
And landslips grin in grey-cream lunacy

Yet the vulture and the skull
Are the alphabet of an oracle:
Here is source, not end

MITOTE OF THE CHAPARRAL

It runs
Where huisache roots pull sunlight
Through sky-hardened ground
To turn it into furry little suns,
It runs

> Grey brown spectre,
> Feathered stick, ugly javelin,
> It runs

Where fading grasses lean
Toward vanished summer
To summon its long-gone honey,
It runs

> Phantom hoofbeats,
> Pilgrim with the rubber
>   laughter,
> It runs

Where heatwaves deform the sun
Into petrified snails on hillslopes
And flat shells of dried lizards,
It runs

> Furtive guardian,
> Roughscaled serpent killer,
> It runs

Where sunlight settles like its own ashes on adobe,
Undriven, unsummoned, undying, unconquered, but haunted
It runs

MITOTE OF THE SCREECH OWL

Voice broken on old night
O ghost

Cry no to the dawn star
Sin-buzzard

Blind moonlight with echoes
Conjure-bird

Tear omens from night's groin
Doom-laughter

Answer the prowling grave,
Name-crier

Shriek away dying
Shriek away pain
Shriek away nightwatchfulness

Demon
Demon
Demon

MITOTE OF THE COYOTE

Ancient voice
Grey brown voice
Lifting on the darkness

       Nightstar
       Falling star
       Hear our outcast brother

Dry wail
Hurting howl
Calling up the moon at full

       Mother moon
       Maize moon
       Hear the longdrawnpain

Hot cry
Chilling cry
Ghost of root and tree

       Old wind
       Cold wind
       Hear the lonely sound

Ancient hurt
Empty night
No home, no trail, no meat

       O rock
       Grey rock
       Hear the spirit breaking

       Let it not break
       O rock

Ha-i-yah!

MITOTE OF THE TUMBLE-BUG

Where are you moving the sun,
Vulture-bug?

> The sun rolls across my sky

Where did you capture the sun,
Buzzard-bug?

> The sun bubbled up out of
>   corruption

Why are you holding the sun,
Juggler-bug?

> The sun stumbles with its
>   richness

Why are you rolling the sun,
Rumble-bug?

> The sun's path makes earth
>   magic

Where will you keep the sun,
Scavenger-bug?

> The sun goes, the sun comes--
> it is not mine

> It is not where it goes,
> but the going that is mine

> And I am looking for a place
> where it can rest

> > No, not here
> > No, not here
> >   Not here
> >   Not here
> >   No

MITOTE OF THE HAWK

Sky
Where are you
When the hawk looks down?

Hills
Where are you
When the hawk watches a rabbit?

Wings
Where are you
When the hawk tears at the fur?

Earth
Where are you
When the hawk becomes a star?

Man
Where are you
When the hawk screams?

MITOTE OF THE MUD-DAUBER

Home is not far, little mother
        Home is everywhere
Earth is there
Earth is here

Build a house, little mother,
Of earth and rain,
With care, little mother, with care,
In air and sun

A broken house lets out the sun
        Hum and dance and wall it in

A broken house lets in the moon
        Hum and dance and wall it out

Home is not far, little mother
        There is no wandering
Earth is here
Water is here

Earth is everyone's cud
        Hum and dance and taste it again
It still tastes like home

MITOTE OF THE WATERBUG

The foot holds the earth
The eye holds the sky
The clay pool holds the sky
    Waterbug
    Doublebug
    Dance on the sky

The wind prowls
The earth stays
The clay pool stays a while

Rain gathers here
It sleeps in the sun
    Waterbug
    Dreamwatcher
    Dance while the sky remains

The pool will dry and crack
The sky will die
    Waterbug waterbug
    Where will you go?

    Your foot holds the earth
    All eyes hold the sky
    My clay pool holds the sky
        I hold the clay pool a while

    What if it slips away?
    The earth stays
    The rain will come again
    The sky pool was made for me

    Can you walk on water?
    Can you dance on the sky?

    There was no sky to dance on
    Before the rain
    You were not here
    I was not here

I dance on the sky while I can
It is my sky to dance on

Take your shadow away

It is summer, waterbug
It will not rain

Yet I will dance on the sky,
Voice of a shadow,
While you lie on the water

I shall dance
I will dance
On the sky till it turns mud

MITOTE OF DESERT GRASS

How many arms are reaching away?
How many fingers are counting the sky?

This quivering green
                    is the hand of a lizard.
That tan skeleton
                    is the hand of a mouse.

Spider webs are rooting here.

Shadows of cobwebs are crawling away.

We are reaching again,
                    arms to the sun.

These are our shadows
but it is our sun.

Ha-i-yah!

MITOTE OF THE WASP NEST

If the place of birth
be a dead place

If the gathered years
be dust to the tongue

If the ancient wind
be a dry whisper

If the grey bell
be a soundless call

If the old home
be mud of ashes

If the lines of earth
be writing

Earth keeps its secret
        Let nothing be abandoned
The lines keep their secret
        Let nothing be lost

Eyes are too brief
to read long signs
        All things go to earth
        Let the earth be the meaning

MITOTE OF THE AGAVE

Drink and hold silence, old spear pile

The dew gathers on your gullied tongues,
The rain slides into your secret places.
Lift the buried rivers

And make spears to keep off the thirsty,
Teeth to saw into flesh for blood,
Turn your plunder into weapons

Tougher than the drouth,
Tougher than the summer sun,
You are alone, old spear pile

Do you dream of birds?
Do you dream of flies?
Do you dream of bees?

You raise spikes against the living,
You gather your own death--
What do you dream?

Your death is a flower--
It seeps through you, waiting.
Drink and hold silence.

Birds and flies and bees will visit your dying,
Old spear pile;
Scorpions and lizards and snakes
Will find shade in your skeleton

Drink as you must, old spear pile,
And hold silence--
You hold no secret the seasons will not tell

Ha-i-yah!

MITOTE OF THE CENTURY PLANT

Among the rasp of dried leaves tugged across the dirt,
    Wait, wait

Near the mesa gathering silence from the hot flat floor,
    Wait, wait

Beneath the freight of the silence of circling birds,
    Wait, wait

With a voice like a dried leaf on a stone, depthless,
    Wait, wait

In a sullen passion, raging thorns onto green shafts,
    Wait, wait

Between valleys haunted by unremembered water,
    Wait, wait

On brown earth gone grey with heat-leached leaves,
    Wait, wait

When night rattles, uncoils, and slithers westward,
    Wait, wait

Though only the demented rain knows how to find more
water,
    Wait, wait

Within unending whirlpools of impenetrable sunlight,
    Wait, wait

While the gray green wine of green recurrence gathers,
    Wait, wait

Wait

MITOTE OF THE RATTLESNAKE

The wind
Unwinds
                    !!
Light coils around stones,
Rough loaves for time's table
                    !!-!!
Stars wink from sinuous curves
Where stones are a broken grin
                    !!-!!-!!
Seed pods rattle in leathered light,
The invisible spider clutching gently
                    !!-!!-!!-!!
Cactus kisses the touch with the murderous delicacy
Of grapevine lightning shaping death with its thunder-
          tongue
                    !!-!!-!!-!!-!!
And the riddling fountain of a spring on a hillside
                    sings of sun apples and the fragile pose
                    of an insect's leg till memory becomes
                    a green vine writhing sunward and poises
                    in sudden silence
                    !!
Flat grey eyes empty themselves of light
And dusty denial drowses in a wicker of flames
                    !!
Then all shadows stumble eastward,
And, wedged among hillstones, a cactus roots
                    !!
The wind
Unwinds and meanders away, migrant among the mesas

MITOTE OF DUSTDEVILS

Turn and hum and sway in the sun
Volcanoes sleep beneath the layered dust
Turn and hum
Mesas drift, clay clouds, in slow seasons
And sway in the sun
The land is thrust up through vanished seas
Turn and hum
The sunlight erodes the iron sole of heaven
And sway in the sun
Hell comes unsummoned with its hunger-heat
Turn and hum
Drouth flicks its scorpion tail at the sky
And sway in the sun
Smoketrees are a purgatory of grey flame leaves
Turn and hum
And heat is a chrysalis, ancient and drowsing
And sway in the sun
And movement is metamorphosis, ancient and lost
Turn and hum and sway in the sun

MITOTE OF YUCCAS BLOOMING

Slow silence finds a sunny knothole onto rocks and tangled
    inland shores

Where silent bells, white from hellish vespers, lift to
    angel-fire, ancient blasting grace

Of the shrieking demon sun whose clamor falls away into
    the mesh of drowsing distance

Where bodiless voices, paused between screams, become
    fluted cups of hot-cream tongues

Whose taproot writhes down to flatrock where water is a
    blind memory awakened by flawless skies

Where 'candles of God,' lamps of silence, pale chalices
    brim with noonday fire

That touches with hard joy the blond-blooming flame-curve
    of wax petals lifting;

And reveals in those lifting curves that sand lies dreaming
    of mating with the sun

MITOTE OF THE BAT

When demons come
They come at nightfall

Their skin is dead
Their faces show their pain

Flying snakes strike the air
        and call to us, call to us

From the mouth of night's great cave
        they call, "Escape, escape"

Do not listen, brothers
Stir the fire
        do not hear them

Demons bring messages
They scratch signs on the sky

        Do not watch them
        Do not read them

To our fires they call,
        "Escape"
They laugh between the canyon walls

        Do not listen

They are demons with the skins of mummies
They are demons with pain whipping their faces

Put more wood on the fire
Tomorrow will come

MITOTE OF THE ACORN

Pretty egg, smooth in the hand

Egg of earthfire, hard green egg
      fullblooded with green anger

It is potent magic, green stone strength,
The bitter of angry vomit

It waits in the hard green egg
It waits in the tough grey tree

When a lizard hatches this yolk of bitter fire
it becomes a hate-tree

      The tree is tough and slow
      It was a long time waiting

      When it hatches it cracks rocks
      Not even the wind can break it down

It is grey from ancient times
It is green from a long time waiting

      It waits
      It is waiting now

Ha-i-yah!

MITOTE OF THE COBWEB

Old blanket gone grey in the dark
Old hands long dead wove it
      Long dead
Blanket to keep off the cold, ragged blanket
Blanket to keep off the wind, thin blanket

Old blanket gone soft
The hard sun will watch a burial tomorrow
      Shelter from the autumn drizzle
      Shelter from the sun at noon

Grave blanket white with smokebrush ashes
False moon indoors, moonlight on adobe floors

The loom is broken and gone
      Burned long ago in the Winter of the Winds
The hands of the weaver are milkweed husks
They are brown gourds spilling dust

Old grey blanket remains
      on the ground, here
there, in a crack where the rock walls rise

      Nightspider makes a web
      The web takes the dew from the night
      The sun takes the dew from the web
      And the spider is gone with the night

Old grey blanket is wet
      It is the dew
And the sun will rise, soon
      The spider is already gone

MITOTE OF THE FIRE-ANT

Ear to earth's belly, listen to the fire-ants

They are humming in the mound, a lullaby
It is a secret singing, listen

In their holes the ants are humming
      to their eggs, to their young

The sound is solid and soft
      with a thousand secret voices

The sound is hot and rounded
They are singing in the mound, a lament

In their secret caves the ants are grieving
They cannot have the sun

Listen, a lullaby, a lament

Hand on the mound, ear to earth's belly,
Listen to the singing
      listen to the secret of the mound

They make the sun with their stings
And they hum in the dark
      It is a lullaby
      It is a lament

MITOTE OF BROOMWEED

Beyond the firelight
　　Back there
All days dry in the sun

　　　　Here is the cooked meat
　　　　Here is the fresh water
　　　　Here is the sleeping place

　　　　　　Make a broom
　　　　　　Use a broom
　　　　　　Make the sign in the dust

Beyond the firelight
　　Ahead there
One more day waits for the sun
　　　　Here is the fire
　　　　Here is the light
　　　　Here is the swept place

　　　　　　Skinny broom
　　　　　　Tough broom
　　　　　　Make the sign in the dust

Old death writes on the sky
　　With a vulture
We write on this earth with a broom

Ha-i-yah!

MITOTE OF THE NOPAL

The green god stands
waiting for the drum to begin,

all hands to the sun,
all hands to the wind.

The green god dances,
the god of greenhands;

the slow dance begins
with a silent scream.

The green god is the hands
earth uses for a tongue--

listen with your eyes--
the music is the sun.

MITOTE OF THE LAUREL BEAN

The sun became a red disk
        on the eyelids
and a drop of blood became a red feather
        on the skin
and a fire-ant became a red jewel
        on a path
and a berry became a red hole
        in a green leaf
and a coal became a red egg
        in the ashes
and a leaf became a red acorn
        by the water
and summer became a laurel bean
        on this tree

Sleep in your shell, hot odor
Be my totem, sleeping wisdom
Sleep in my hand, hot secret
Be my necklace, sleeping fire

Sleep through the winter, summer sun

MITOTE OF THE MESQUITE BEAN

Autumn earth is nutsweet
ripe to foot and hand
ripe to nose and eye

But ghosts come here,
ghost voices, ghost hands

The curved pods speak
when nothing else moves

        Answer with the clacksticks,
        Speak, speak, speak

The pink pods whisper
when the air is still

        Answer with the seed gourds,
        Speak, speak, speak

Ghost hands stroke the stored sweetness
when there is no wind

        Answer with the rattles,
        Speak, speak, speak

Shadows grow pale,
the day dies, the moon wanes,
the year grows old

And ghosts reveal their presence,
ghost voices, ghost hands

The wasp nest is empty,
everything is leaving.
Only ghosts remain

        And, walking around us,
        Speak, speak, speak

And earth is nutsweet
with long drawn beans
that shiver in the sun

   Answer with a campfire--
   Ghosts may be cold

MITOTE OF THE SCORPION

Earth-silence is a dance
       Dance the silence
       Dance the silence of stones
              Leap, fire,
              Leap soon

A brown man
Waiting still as stone
In the noon sun
       Is dancing
              Fire, leap soon

A brown tree
Standing still as stone
In the hot air
       Is dancing
              Fire, leap soon

A brown leaf
Poised still as stone
On the dry earth
       Is dancing
              Fire, leap soon

Earth-lightning is a dance
       Dance the fire
       Dance the leaping of fire
              Leap, fire
              Soon, fire
              Soon, soon

MITOTE OF THE MOURNING DOVE

There is no home
        Anywhere
We are on the way
        Somewhere, nowhere

Wherever we are
We hear from far off, over there somewhere,
The sound of loneliness,
The voice of somewhere else
        Hillside voice
        Canyon voice
        Cedar voice
            Somewhere, nowhere
        Voice of evening
        Voice on the wind
        Voice of empty places
            Somewhere, nowhere

There is no home
        Anywhere
We rest on the way
From somewhere to somewhere else
And night is coming
        Everywhere

MITOTE OF THE CAT-CLAW VINE

Pain in the flesh tears outward

An old foot walks in the dust
and leaves no trail

Fangs of green tear at our feet

A twig brush paints old pots
and leaves no sign

Pain in the head tears outward

A rawhide pouch carries the flint
and leaves no heat

Claws of green hold us back

The autumn rain douses old campfires
and leaves no coals

Pain in the chest tears outward

The old one's hand holds the past
and leaves no mark

The old pain in the groin tears outward

The old one's hand holds the land,
the old one's head holds the past

       How can we hold the old one?

The sun goes down.
We hold on till it is gone

Green vines try to snag the wind

       Night comes

Ha-i-yah!

MITOTE OF SUMMER THUNDER

The cloud
is a grey cloud
the color of stones,
old stones

Its voice
is an old voice

Pile a stone
on a stone

The voice
is a dry voice

Pile two stones
on two stones

The wind
is a prowling wind

Pile some stones
on some stones

The voice
is a lonely voice

Pile more stones
on more stones

The wind
is a waiting wind

The stones
shift, the stones
grind and clatter, the stones
pound and fall and roll, the stones
rumble to the dust

The drum
is a muffled drum

The voice
is a tired voice,
the voice
of old stone.

MITOTE OF THE EVENING STAR

Come, Evening Star

The air grows thin
The air grows still
Cold sets in

Shine, Evening Star

Darkness gathers
Brother Cricket starts singing
Soon, night

Hear Brother Cricket
He is singing for you
Sing for us, Evening Star

The fire spits stars
The green wood sings
Night sets in

See the campfire
It is our star for you
Shine for us, Evening Star

Night is here
It is cold
The fire glows like the old moon

You are going, Evening Star
Why do you come when we call?
What is to be remembered
When you leave us?

Brother Cricket goes on singing
In the dark when you leave--
Is he blind?
Is he afraid?
Is he wise?

Brother Cricket
the Evening Star is gone
Come sing to our dying fire

MITOTE OF THE LIZARD

Drowsing eyes too old to blink, watching;
old hands dry like weeds
on hot flat stones

Wrinkled face too gray to change, waiting;
old skin like dry leaves
on hot rough earth

Stiff body too hot to move, waiting;
on a ledge of rock brown grey
with the heat of old suns

Dried old body, faded old lizard,
watching and waiting;
desert mildew, waiting
for all color to die,
waiting to be king of grey,

Old eyes, old sun, look somewhere else--
            Bodies are not grey

Gray face, gray stone, do not wait--
            Living things are not grey

Those eyes make ashes
of everything they see

Those old eyes watching

Look away, old eyes

MITOTE OF THE MOTTE

Two trees, three trees, four trees, a motte

On a still day
a tribe of silences
watches the horizon

Beyond the hills, canyons wait,
counting the years

As night stalks in
a council of winds
draws itself into a circle

The hills camp at a distance
where noises prowl

> Tomorrow will never come here
> Yesterday has never been here
> Here, it is always today
> Here, it is always now

Two trees, three trees, four trees, a motte

The land reaches away on every side
The eye is lonely
The ear is lonely

A snake or a storm
or an enemy would be welcome

And song dies in the chest,
even Tree Songs will not take root

MITOTE OF THE SNAKE-SKIN

Sunlight has fallen away
    Go sun, dark sun,
    Come fire
Darkness gathers
    In the dark, come fire

The heat of the flames
Pushes into the face
It makes moonlight in the darkness
    In the dark, come fire

Dancing phantoms rise
In the flames,
Presences in its moonlight
    Fire, Father Fire

The darkness splits its skin against the firestones
And firelight works its way out
It lies panting in the wind

The snake sheds its skin,
    Fire, Father Fire,
The night sheds its skin
Take the Snake-Skin, Father fire,
    Burn it, burn it
Let all skins be shed

Dancing phantoms touch the face
The flames are dying
Darkness coils around the fire
    and hisses and hisses

Its skin is new and black

MITOTE OF THE ECHO

They are here,
the presences
        Ha-i-yah!
They are everywhere

They move
like the heart
of a dustdevil

They watch
with eyes
like cracks in canyon ledges

They call
like crickets
in the time of the cheese moon
        Ha-i-yah!

They touch
like shadows,
        fire shadow and moon shadow

They leave no trail
They leave no campfire
They leave no bones for ants to clean

They are there,
the presences,
They are everywhere

Listen, they are nearby,
        listen,
Listen, they are over there
        Ha-i-yah!
         i-yah
         i-yah
Listen, they are listening

MITOTE OF THE MESA

Table of the gods

Here is a feast of air
              when insects dance
Here is a feast of sun
              when every stone is a cookstone

Here is a jerky of moon
              when the fire hunches down
              into its blanket of ashes

Here is the food offering
              to the sun sky, moon sky
Ha-i-yah!

Everything is food for offering
Everything is food
              for the table of the gods

The gods are hungry
They eat the life of things
The gods are patient
They eat all things

Here they eat the offering song
They eat until the bones of silence show

The table of the gods is silent

They are silent now
They are hungry now
They are patient

              Ha-i-yah!

When the gods are hungry
All things are venison

MITOTE OF THE ANT-MOUND

In the dark there are secrets,
run and hide

In the tunnels where earth odors hide
there are secrets

The sign made by cut-leaf trails
is your secret

Only ants read its warning,
and run and hide

Your caves are ghost fingers
of old earth

In a sign of secret presence,
and you hum

You hum in your caves, you hum power,
you hum secrets

You strip a tree, you strip a carcass--
you peel the soft shell

From earth eggs, and you hum
the slow hard hatching

Do your signs tell you what will hatch?
why do you run?

Why do you hide, why do you hum?
Do you hum a sign?

Unending song where the sun never goes.
Mighty ant

MITOTE OF THE GOURD

The green earthsnake
has laid its green eggs,
   poison green, green poison,
and has nested them in leaves,
   a long time coiling

The yellow earthsnake
has uncovered its yellow eggs,
   poison yellow, yellow poison,
and has nested them in sunlight,
   a long time brooding

The brown earthsnake
has left its brown eggs,
   dead brown, creekstone brown,
and has died, belly up,
   a long time dying

Twilight air is an earthsnake,
   a tough vine coiling,
making leaves to cover the earth
a snake egg brooding and hatching in the sun,
   the egg of the skysnake

The brown earth will hatch

   Ha-i-yah!

The yellow sun will hatch

   Ha-i-yah!

And all green vines will die,
   a long time dying

   Ha-i-yah!

MITOTE OF THE COWSKULL

Sister Skull, what are you waiting for?
> *The sun*

The sun will not come, Sister Skull.
> *I can wait--the sun will tire*

Sister Skull, what are you waiting for?
> *The seasons*

The seasons are slow, Sister Skull.
> *I can wait--the seasons return*

Sister Skull, what are you waiting for?
> *The sunset*

The sunset is far off, Sister Skull.
> *I can wait--the sunset crawls toward me*

> *Bone is patient beyond seasons,*
> *Wisdom is in the bone,*
> *Bone is the long white silence,*
> *Silence knows everything,*
> *And bone can wait*

Sister Skull, what are you waiting for?
> *You*

But I am free to go, Sister Skull.
> *I can wait--*
> *Scavengers reveal the god*
> *And all things come home*